Basic Buddhism Through Comics

by **Mitsutoshi Furuya**

Rissho Kosei-kai International of North America

Basic Buddhism Through Comics

This book was originally published in Japan in 1998 under the title *Manga Konpon Bukkyo* by Kosei Publishing Company. The original Japanese edition was published under the editorial supervision of the Education Group of Rissho Kosei-kai and with the editorial assistance of Chijinkan.

Translated from the Japanese by Rissho Kosei-kai International.

Published in English in 2009 by Rissho Kosei-kai International of North America, 4255 Campus Drive, Suite A-245, Irvine, CA 92612, U.S.A. All rights reserved.

ISBN: 978-0-9842044-0-3

Prologue
Reaffirm the Self, and Live in the Universal Truth
(Self-Reliance, Reliance on the Dharma)

The crow caws, and a new year is born.

I hope this is another good year.

I do too. So let's get cracking on "Basic Buddhism."

By "Basic Buddhism," do you mean "Lotus Sutra" Buddhism?

Yes, they both bring happiness to people through their teachings.

1

Basic Buddhism is a collection of major concepts from all the Buddhist teachings.

Knowing these key elements will help you study the Lotus Sutra.

I see. They are like "stepping-stones."

Right. Let's start with Self-Reliance and Reliance on the Dharma.

法灯明 自灯明

Sounds pretty reliable.

First, let's look back at ancient India.

From now on, let yourself and the Dharma

illuminate your practice of the teachings.

Shakyamuni Buddha, when you, the World Honored One, pass away, how should we continue our practice of the teachings?

Hmmm. And that was Buddha's final teaching?

Don't you see the big picture?

Not one bit!

Well, let's take a look at the world of people...

Tomorrow, take the long way to work, approaching from the east, and you will meet with good fortune.

Stop worrying about such trifles!

STOP!

I have lots of good luck, you know.

Really? How'd you manage that?

I found a fortune-teller who's always right, and she helps me with my work and personal relationships.

I know this priest who's done some incredible training.
With just one session he can make you feel like a new person.

Wow, we both found two great people.

a while later

...

What's wrong? You don't seem very happy lately.

Well, I noticed you've been sort of blue lately, too.

The thing is... my priest has gone away to do some more training.

Oh... what a selfish priest!

You're right. My problems keep growing while he's gone.

And my fortune-teller's really sick, so I can't get advice anymore.

Now we're in trouble.

You got that right.

4

These two have a problem on their hands.

That's because they are too dependent on other people.

So the lesson is "rely on yourself"?

That's right, be your own light.

You might be okay for a while relying on others, but you'll never truly be at peace.

"Taking one's own path," eh?

In that case, just leave it to me!

I'll do what I want, when I want, how I want...

That's just plain selfishness!

OW!

The "path" refers to a path of spiritual training, which you yourself must pursue!

Now take a look at this:

...

He is a fine speaker, but he never follows his own advice.

You can't take him seriously.

And he's always bugging us to lead our neighbors to the faith, but when we try, they aren't interested.

With him around, who feels like doing any training?

You see? Their blaming others becomes an excuse not to try any more.

They aren't truly self-reliant, in other words?

Right. Be responsible for the path you choose to take.

But trying to free yourself from earthly desires all by yourself isn't the answer either, is it?

That's where Reliance on the Dharma comes in.

We've been relying on the law of Mogura, Wide-Illuminating Mole god, since ancient times.

Can you really find inner peace in something like that - something outside of yourself? And what's a mole doing on a tree branch?

?

I forgot to make offerings to Mogura and now I'm worried that an earthquake or something bad might happen.

Well, what do you expect. You'll never find inner peace that way...

Reliance on the Dharma teaches us that we must live our lives according to the Universal Truth.

I got to thinking and...maybe we shouldn't have depended on other people for advice.

Come to think of it, you're right. We've got to pull ourselves together here.

I don't really like him, but at least what what he says is right.

He shares the teachings as the Buddha intended.

We can't deny that, even if we don't like him.

After all, what really matters are the teachings.

You're right, we should accept what he says gratefully, the same as the words of the Buddha himself.

It's good to see everyone so happy.

Grandpa, this Universal Truth must be pretty tough to learn.

That's where the Buddha comes in. His teachings make it easy for everyone to comprehend.

Let's go on to the next chapter.

So let's get started...and that goes for everybody out there too.

Buddhagaya, the Land of Buddha's Enlightenment

Index

Prologue
Reaffirm the Self, and Live in the Universal Truth
(Self-reliance, Reliance on the Dharma) ··· 1

Basic Buddhist Teachings
(The Three Seals of the Dharma)

All Things Are Impermanent ··· 13
Nothing Has a Separate Self ··· 21
Nirvana Is Quiescence ··· 29

Seeing the World Through Causation
(The Dharma of Causation) ··· 37

The Truth that Rids Suffering, Gives Hope, and Unleashes Courage (The Four Noble Truths)

Truth of Suffering ··· 45
Truth of Cause 1 ··· 53
Truth of Cause 2: Ten Suchnesses ··· 61
Truth of Cause 3: Ten Realms of Being Found in One Another ·········· 69
Truth of Path, Truth of Extinction ··· 77
**Truth of Cause 4: The Dharma of Twelve Causes and
                           Conditions** ··· 85
The Four Noble Truths (Conclusion) ··· 93

The Eight Precepts for Spiritual Growth (The Eightfold Path)

Right View, Right Thought · 101
Right Speech, Right Action · 109
Right Livelihood, Right Effort, Right Mindfulness,
Right Concentration · 117

Six Paramitas That Lead to Spiritually Rich Living (Six Practices)

Donation 1 · 125
Donation 2 · 133
Precept-keeping and Forbearance · 141
Diligence, Meditation and Wisdom · 149

Review of the Teachings of Buddha

Applying the Teachings to Real Life 1 · 157
Applying the Teachings to Real Life 2 · 165
Applying the Teachings to Real Life 3 · 173
Overall Review · 181

Epilogue
Three Guideposts in Life
(Taking Refuge in the Three Treasures) · 189

Sarnath, the Land of the First Rolling of the Dharma-wheel

Basic Buddhist Teachings
(The Three Seals of the Dharma)
All Things Are Impermanent

In this chapter we will be learning the Three Seals of the Dharma, considered the most fundamental of the Buddha's teachings.

And what are the three?

All things are impermanent, nothing has a separate self, and nirvana is quiescence.

"The tolling of the bell of Jetavana Vihara echoes the impermanence of all things."

That's a very famous, yet difficult, poem you memorized there.

Doesn't it mean that life is short and empty?

Tsk, tsk. Your comprehension's not quite on par with your memory

Really? What does it mean then?

Well, let's learn the teaching of All things are impermanent by people-watching...

I swear, the people in this house just don't get it!

My husband can't seem to get promoted at work and when he's home he just lies around.

All my son does is play video games instead of doing his homework.

And ...

What my daughter does locked up in her room all day is anybody's guess!

Stay Out!

Nobody In this family ...

has a clue!

I'm going out for a while!

And all Mom does is nag!

My family is beyond help.

You shouldn't say that.

I've already given up on them.

Don't say that. After all, you're the mother, you should try harder.

But no matter how much I try, they never change!

Well, the Buddha taught

that all phenomena definitely change.

That might be true in theory, but the real world's a different thing.

Well, are you okay with how things are now?

Of course not!

Well then, have faith in the Buddha's teachings, and just do your best.

What exactly should I do?

Don't assume all's lost...try stepping into their shoes for a change.

All right. I'll give it another try.

I'm rooting for you. Good luck!

Thanks!

Dear, in the beginning, you were such a go-getter at work, but these days you seem less enthusiastic.

At work, they only promote the boss's relatives or people with fancy degrees.

They'll never consider me.

Well, promotion can't be the only thing to look forward to at work, dear.

Hey! You're the one always nagging me about getting a promotion.

Say, you're right! Well, from now on I won't mention it.

There's something different about you today, Mom.

That's right. Everything in this world continues to change, you know!

Not me. Like father, like son. I'll never be any good at school.

Doing well at school's not the only thing in life.

You're the one constantly nagging me about my homework!

How about those fairy tales you like to write?

I prefer the term "fantasy novel," thank you very much.

When you write a new one, I'd like to read it.

Did something happen Mom? You're all smiles today.

I got some great advice from a friend of mine. "In this world, everything changes."

Not me. I take after my parents. That's why I'll never be popular.

Sorry you take after me, honey.

17

But even if you only say "Hi" to people, they will like you.

There's definitely something strange about you today...

What kind of story should I write this time?

Already at work on a new story?

Yeah, but I didn't know how to spell a word, so I've just been flipping through the dictionary.

It's pretty important to know your spelling, isn't it?

It sure is.

tweet

tweet

Good morning!

Ah, morning.

Morning!

Oh, um, morning!

and after one week

Mom! Look at my score on this English test!

Wow, better than usual!

18

But look, on spelling I got a perfect score!

And your other subjects are good, too.

I understand the questions better now.

Your fairy tale hobby is really paying off.

That's "novels," Mom.

Mom, guess what! I've been invited to a friend's birthday party.

Oh, so you made some friends, huh?

Will you buy me something nice to wear?

Let's go shopping soon.

I'm home ~!!

Hey, what's with all the smiles?

Everyone certainly has cheered up.

All the neighbors have been telling me how much happier you seem recently, dear.

And Mom hasn't been her usual nagging self, either.

Basic Buddhist Teachings
(The Three Seals of the Dharma)
Nothing Has a Separate Self

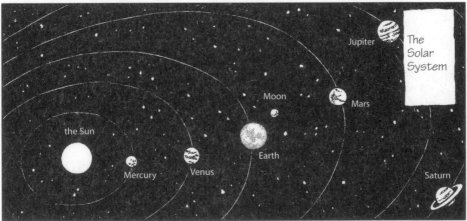

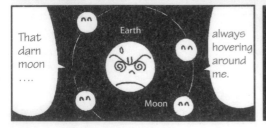

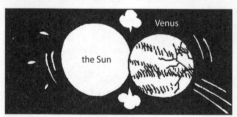

The chain reaction that followed destroyed one planet after another...

even the sun was destroyed.

Only the earth managed to avoid the chaos.

Phew, that was close...
It's a good thing I was spared.

Hey, the sun's gone!

I better get out of here!

ZOOM~!

Ahh!

What's the matter!? Why did you scream?

I had this terrible dream.

Oh, sounds like it was almost the end of the world.

No more dreams about me being the earth.

But that dream might just help us with our next lesson, "Nothing Has a Separate Self."

"Nothing has a separate self?" What does that mean?

That nothing in this world stands alone: in some way, everything is connected to everything else.

Hmmm. How so?

Well, let's take a look at the world of humans to find out.

Dinner's ready, kids!

I'm eating out with my friends tonight, Mom.

I'll eat as soon as I finish writing this...

Dad's been coming home late these days.

Oh well. And I have to leave pretty soon.

I'll just wrap it up, so he can eat it when he gets home.

Everybody's been doing their own thing recently.

Even the neighbors have noticed.

Have you been able to sit down as a family and have dinner together lately?

No. But no one seems to mind.

Do you know the expression "Nothing has a separate self?"

What's that?

The belief that all things in the universe are connected, and nothing exists in and of itself.

Hmm…

In other words, nobody lives only by their own power…in fact, we are all caused to live by everything else in this world.

Does that have anything to do with my family?

Of course! The family, the foundation of our personal relationships, is caused to live by everything around us.

...

That's why we are supported and influenced by the world around us.

I never thought of it that way...

It's fine to be passionate about something you like, but you can't always do as you please.

What should I do then?

Realize that since your actions influence the people around you, it's best to live unselfishly and nurture your personal relationships.

I'll have to give that some serious thought later tonight.

I'm home!

Welcome back! You sure look happy today. Something good happen at work?

Remember the other day, when you were saying "getting promoted at work isn't everything"?

Yeah, I remember.

I stopped thinking about getting a promotion. Instead, I asked the boss to let me develop a new area.

Really? So that's why you've been so busy lately

I went around to what must've been a hundred companies before one finally showed interest in my idea.

That's great, honey!

And it just so happens that the boss of that company knows my boss.

Aha~

All things in the universe are connected.

My boss said that it was a great idea, because then we'll be able to set up a new department just for this new area.

That's great! It's definite all things in the universe are connected. So, nothing has a separate self.

And in fact, I'm the one they put in charge of this new department.

You're Department Manager now?

Well, just Assistant Manager, to be exact.

several days later

I'm home.

What's wrong dear?

Everybody's saying it's my fault we lost the soccer match.

Well, come to think of it, you haven't been going to practice very often, have you?

It doesn't really matter if one person doesn't show up to practice!

A friend told me that everything in this world is interconnected.

What's that supposed to mean?

It means that not going to practice and improving your soccer isn't just your own problem. It affects other people, too.

When you put it that way, I guess you're right.

Remember, it's not just soccer, either. If you are slacking off, you are letting others down.

I guess I should stop thinking only about myself.

It's been a while since we all had dinner together.

Here's to Dad's promotion.

It took some time, but even Dad changed for the better!

The effort paid off - just like Mom said it would!

And even I've gotten busy with soccer and homework!

But don't forget: Sunday the whole family has dinner together.

You betcha!

And it's all thanks to our wonderful mother.

And I owe it all to the Dharma.

So as you can see, what really makes us happy is leading our lives with gratitude for the gift of life and trying to repay our debt for that.

But it sure looks like a lot of work.

Of course! "Progress on the road of life comes only with effort" is a key Buddhist teaching.

Sounds a bit out of my league.

With that attitude you'll never stop having those bad dreams...like the one about the sun exploding.

Anything but that!

28

Basic Buddhist Teachings
(The Three Seals of the Dharma)
Nirvana Is Quiescence

All the teachings of the Buddha evolved from the Three Seals of the Dharma. The meaning of "Nirvana is quiescence" is simply the state of total peacefulness that comes when one realizes the truth of the first two seals:

"All things are impermanent" and "Nothing has a separate self." In contrast, when we do not understand these two truths and are deluded by our own thoughts, we are in a state of total suffering, which in Buddhism is called "All things are suffering."

We've now completed our study of the first two seals: "All things are impermanent" and "Nothing has a separate self."

All things change, and all things are interconnected.

Yep.

So what's the third one?

Now hold on there... First answer this –

What?

What was the family like, before they learned of the first two seals?

...

They are so stubborn!

No matter how much I try, they just won't change!

There's no way I'll ever get a promotion at my job!

I'll never be smart enough to do well in school.

Nobody will ever hang out and be friends with me.

It doesn't matter if one guy skips soccer practice!

They were an irritable and pathetic bunch.

They certainly didn't feel fulfilled.

In other words, when people don't understand that all things are impermanent and that nothing has a separate self, they end up quarreling with each other. This is the meaning of "All things are suffering."

I get it! So the third Seal must be "All things are suffering!"

Tsk, tsk. Don't jump ahead just yet. First answer this question: How exactly did the family change after incorporating the first two seals into their daily lives?

Umm....

Yeah, now I understand the questions better.

Your fairy tale hobby actually paid off!

Hey Mom! I got invited to a birthday party!

Oh, you made some friends, did you?

Dad, your effort paid off, just like Mom said it would!

Everyone's pretty happy now.

Exactly. This is the quiescence of nirvana, complete inner peace.

...

Why so quiet?

Will you tell me again if I say "The third seal is 'Nirvana is quiescence'"?

Nope... you're right this time.

You're not just making fun of me?

I would never do such a thing. "All Things are impermanent," "Nothing has a separate self," and "Nirvana is quiescence," are the Three Seals of the Dharma.

So why were you talking about "All things are suffering" a few minutes ago?

Because it is the opposite of "Nirvana is quiescence," and when included into the Three Seals of the Dharma, it actually becomes the Fourth Seal of the Dharma.

I see. So things get better when we understand the first two seals, and worse if we don't.

That's one way to put it.

But I'm still not being very clear, huh?

The real world's a complicated place, you know. For instance, look at these humans.

Hey, that's the wrong way to swing!

Darn!

I told you so.

Perhaps you could give me a demonstration, then.

First, you have to get your feet in the right place.

Put the ball slightly off-center . . .

Keep your elbow bent at the peak . . .

The bar's closed for the night.

I drank too much again.

I'm sure he's not the only one like that.

In other words, knowing isn't enough.

But if you know it, why can't you do it?

The cause lies deep within the human heart, I'm afraid.

Could you be a little more specific please, Grandpa?

Deep in the human heart lie impulses, that is, the selfish desire to do as they wish.

I see. And are some selfish desires just too deeply rooted to remove?

Yes. Like that family - they may seem OK for now, but if the selfishness returns, they'll be right back where they started again.

Well that's a downer.

Don't worry. The Buddha's teachings include practical methods on how to eliminate this kind of selfishness.

What kind of methods?

The Eightfold Path and the Six Paramitas, to name just two.

Oh…

Later on, we can study them one by one.

Why don't we study them now?

Because first, we must learn about the principles governing this universe, which show us the results of our actions.

The principles governing this universe?

Right. It's called the Dharma of Causation, and it's a very important principle.

And by studying it, everybody can be even happier, right?

And it's all thanks to our wonderful Mother!

And I owe it all to the Dharma!

I suppose so.

"I suppose so?" You don't sound very sure.

It's great to see this family is happy, but there's an even deeper understanding to the teaching of "Nirvana is quiescence."

Sounds like I've still got a lot to learn.

Just take it step by step, one thing at a time

The next chapter is "The Dharma of Causation"

Seeing the World Through Causation
The Dharma of Causation

All things have "causes," and when causes meet with certain "conditions" this leads to a certain "effect."

This "effect" in turn goes on to influence the existence of things around it (recompense).

So, next let's study the Dharma of Causation.

Oh, you can ask me anything about that.

That's quite a confident attitude.

First, "beauty isn't *caused*, it is."

Huh?

Next, "bitter pills have good effects."

What in the world are you talking about?

I'm talking about "causes" and "effects."

Tsk, tsk. Those are just proverbs!

So what kind of causes are we talking about?

The Dharma of Causation means seeing that everything in this world is the effect of previous causes, in other words, it is correctly understanding the Dharma of Causation.

I see. Like causation is insufficient to create liability?

No, no, no!

I give up then!

In simplest terms, there's a cause for everything and when applied to certain conditions a new effect is created, which goes on to affect things around it.

That's not very easy to understand, though.

Well then, let's look at causation in more concrete terms. Take the family:

Everyone seems to be happy.

And how did they get that way?

Well, let's see.

I'll give it another try.

Good morning!

How was that spelled again?

I asked the boss to let me develop a new area.

All of them made some sort of effort.

Exactly. And as an effect, they've become happier.

So, make an effort and things get better!

Things aren't quite that simple. Let's take a look behind the scenes at that family's happiness, shall we?

I'm sorry to say, but there's just no hope for my family!

If you don't change, then neither will your family. Change your attitude, stop assuming they are hopeless, and try stepping into their shoes.

Thanks. I'll give it a try.

I take after my parents. That's why I'll never be popular.

This is where I usually say, "Don't blame me if you're unpopular," but that's no good.

Sorry you take after me, dear. But even if you only say "Hi" to people, they will like you.

All right, but there's definitely something different about you today, Mom.

Good morning!

Ah, morning.

Once you try it, it's easy!

Morning!

Hey, morning.

She's actually pretty nice.

Hey Mom, guess what! I got invited to a birthday party!

Is that so? You made some new friends then?

I'm glad everybody's changed for the better.

Changing MY attitude is what really made a difference. I'm glad, too.

Do you get it now?

By changing the way she dealt with her daughter, the mother improved the parent-child relationship, and brought happiness to the household.

Yep. She (the cause) realized her instinctual habits were not helpful, and by changing the way she dealt with her daughter (the condition), this led to an improved relationship (effect) which further led to kinder feelings all around (recompense).

I got it, Grandpa.

Alright, how about some practical exercises then?

What is this, school?

Let's look at the Dharma of Causation through the example of this tree.

ah!

This tree started off as a tiny seed.

The cause.

And with the right amount of water and sunlight...

The condition

...it becomes the large tree you see now.

The effect.

Without which, we wouldn't have anything to perch upon and rest our wings.

It influences our lives.

So getting back to the family...for argument's sake, what would've happened if the mother had never given up her self-centered attitude?

She most likely would've rejected her friend's well-principled guidance and fallen into even deeper frustration.

Her new attitude is the cause which brought about the happy effect. In other words, even if the condition didn't change, the effect would be different because of the mother's change of heart (cause).

Whoa, deep.

That's what is meant by "Good deeds lead to good results, and bad deeds to bad results."

So the problem lies in the cause, huh?

Now, let's assume a new family, an unhappy bunch, moves in next door to our "happy family."

What? The Dharma of Causation doesn't end with the family becoming happy?

We've only covered as far the "effect." This time our happy family will become the condition for change in the family next door.

There's no end in sight...

42

Our world is constantly changing based on the principles of cause and effect.

That's awfully similar to the first Seal of the Dharma: "All things are impermanent."

And thanks to the positive condition of our happy family, there's hope for the neighbors now, too.

By looking at things this way, you really come to appreciate the complex interaction between cause and condition.

Right. Everything in this world is connected by a vast network of cause, condition, effect and influence.

"Nothing has a separate self."

You're getting it now. In fact, we ourselves are only here thanks to positive conditions.

You mean, I'm understanding The Dharma of Causation, right?

Yes, and with that understanding, we come one step closer to "Nirvana is quiescence."

Just like that family.

Like I said before... what they did still is not quite enough.

Huh?

A more wonderful nirvana is found in leading a positive, meaningful life – that is, not only trying to attain happiness for yourself, but resolving to bring happiness to many.

I suppose you're right...it isn't enough to just be happy by yourself.

Therefore that family must evolve and reach the next level.

I really understand the concept of causation.

Excellent! Next time, we'll study the training you need to reach the next level.

Look out! A black cat is crossing our path! Serious bad luck!

Looks like you're going to need lots of training...

The Truh that Rids Suffering, Gives Hope, and Unleashes Courage (Four Noble Truths)

Truth of Suffering

What is the Dharma gateway called the Four Noble Truths? In this case, Truth means to clarify, to clearly understand these are the Dharmic truths that eradicate the suffering and worry we face in our daily lives, and lead us into a realm of absolute tranquility.

The Truth of Suffering is to look into the actual condition of suffering and worry.
The Truth of Cause is to reflect upon and find the root cause of suffering, and fully realize it.
The Truth of Path is to practice the bodhisattva way, in order to eliminate suffering.
The Truth of Extinction is the realm of tranquility in which suffering and worry are extinguished.

Four Noble Truths (Truth of Suffering)

Thank you all for coming.

In Buddhism, we hear a lot about the Four Noble Truths.

We learn to correct the root of suffering in our daily life,

and develop a peaceful state of mind.

The Four Noble Truths clarify the truths of suffering,

the cause, the extinction, and the path.

It is easy to say,

but hard to do.

Yes?

Oh! Hachi. What are you doing?

Well, Mrs. Kuma is hesitant to come in.

Oh! Mrs. Kuma is with you?

Yes, but she is shy.

Don't be shy. Come on in.

How are you? It's been a while...

 Are you kidding? Didn't I see you yesterday?

Well, it has been a long time since I saw you yesterday.

 What she's saying doesn't make sense.

Grandpa! She is having problems with Mr. Kuma. So I brought her to you for advice.

 If that's the case...

Come on in.

 There's nothing to worry about.

OK.

 Everyone in the world wants peace. That's why you should get the Nobles.

What? You think I want a Nobel Peace Prize!?

No, no. He means, "Be noble if you want to get a piece of the world."

 Nothing like that. It is too bad that you are both in the dark about this. I am talking about the Four Noble Truths.

 Oh?

 They are four gateways to the Dharma, that is, the Buddha's teachings.

Four Noble Truths

People usually want a quick fix, so they skip over the Truth of Suffering to get to the final three.

I am just like that, too.

This isn't Chutes and Ladders, you know. There are no short-cuts.

First off, find the true nature of the problem: Who? what? and how?

I understand! Now, please tell us about your problem.

Well, actually it's my husband's problem.

What's happened to him?

His bad habit started again.

Mr. Kuma is a bad fellow, isn't he, Grandpa?

Hachi! We haven't heard the whole story yet.

It's his drinking. Lately he's drinking every day. I'm worried about his health.

Yes, everyone knows that Mr. Kuma likes to drink...

When he comes home drunk, he complains about his job and yells at the kids.

Oh, that must be hard on your kids.

The next day, he is too hung-over to go to his job as a carpenter.

That is bad.

Yes. He's becoming a problem for his foreman.

By the way, who is suffering? Mrs. Kuma? The kids? Mr. Kuma's boss?

I think all of them are.

Well, in that case, please bring whoever is suffering here. Mrs. Kuma, you are not suffering, so you don't need to be here.

Don't say that! She is worried, you know.

The Truth of Suffering means nothing if the sufferers don't acknowledge their own suffering.

Grandpa!

I am suffering!

So I want you to tell me how YOU are suffering. You don't need to use your husband or your kids as a pretext…

Oh, I'm sorry.

You're the one who is suffering.

My husband isn't working so he doesn't bring home money. He won't even look me in the face lately.

Of course it's hard on his foreman and the kids, but it's hardest on me.

Indeed! He doesn't bring home money, he drinks, and then he gripes at you, doesn't he?

That's right. He is impossible.

OK. Now, I understand how you are suffering from your husband's behavior. I clearly see your suffering.

Mr. Kuma's being unfair to her, Grandpa. Go give him a piece of your mind!

I would give Mr. Kuma advice if he came to me asking for it, but this is his wife's problem right now.

What? But isn't Mr. Kuma the bad guy?

She is the one who is suffering here,

First, let's clarify her suffering and then, in the second stage, we'll search for the cause of suffering and then finally, she can practice the Truth of Path which leads into the Truth of Extinction. These are the teachings of the Four Noble Truths.

Please continue to guide me.

All this talk about the Truth of Extinction and the Truth of Suffering has me confused, Grandpa.

Just because I'm a comedian, don't take this story lightly.

In the real world there are people who don't acknowledge their suffering.

There are those who give up without trying

and those who try to run away from suffering, only to fall into deeper suffering.

In these cases, one needs to squarely face the problem, not make some half-hearted escape.

Just like Grandpa said,

"We must look deeply into the who, what, and how of the suffering."

Four Noble Truths
(Truth of Suffering)

Now that Mrs. Kuma has looked squarely at her own suffering, she can search for the cause of her suffering.

Next comes the Truth of Cause, but this is enough for today.

The Truh that Rids Suffering, Gives Hope, and Unleashes Courage (Four Noble Truths)
Truth of Cause 1

Four Noble Truths (Truth of Cause)

Thank you all for coming to my performance again.

Last time, I talked about the Truth of Suffering, one of the Four Noble Truths.

The Truth of Suffering is discovering the who, what, how, and the true source of suffering.

Last time, we saw that Mrs. Kuma was suffering from her husband's drinking problem.

This time, we learn the Truth of Cause, which reveals the cause of her suffering.

Well, I'd better explain about the the Dharma of Causation before we look into the cause of Mrs. Kuma's suffering.

All right, I will do whatever you tell me to, even if I have to walk on my hands!

Hey, you better not make her walk on her hands!

No more bad jokes, you guys, or our readers won't take us seriously.

We apologize.

Ready to begin? Everything in this world has a cause.

When that cause comes into contact with a condition, an effect is produced. This is called the Dharma of Causation.

You reminded me of a magazine I saw, *Dharma World* or something like that.

Of course, everyone knows that, even the birds in the trees.

ACHOO~

...

By the way, Grandpa, what is the connection between the Dharma of Causation and the Truth of Cause?

That is a good question.

According to the Dharma of Causation, nothing happens by accident. There is no result without a cause.

Then my suffering has a cause – is that what you're saying?

Of course. Mr. Kuma's drinking is the source of her suffering, isn't it?

Hold on, Hachi, I can't tell you what the real cause of her suffering is until I listen to her story from beginning to end.

Why bother? I can tell you what's wrong right now.

When something happens it has numerous causes, so many that you can hardly pinpoint a single cause.

That's right. There are so many things I want to say, but I don't know where to start.

You shouldn't over-concern yourself with indirect causes (conditions).

The direct cause, which is the major force at work when something happens, is called the real cause.

Grandpa, please tell me more.

Well, I want to hear about your problem in detail.

OK.

When did Mr. Kuma start drinking?

From the beginning of our marriage, he always liked to drink, but it never got out of hand.

Oh, did he talk with you a lot back then?

He is a man of few words, like any carpenter. He looked after the kids when they were toddlers.

He must be kindhearted…

You know, he talks a lot when he is drunk, even nowadays.

What does he talk about?

Mostly he just gripes.

 He says that he wants to do a good job, but his foreman wants the job done before the deadline.

 The foreman worries about paying overtime. My husband complained about the same thing over and over, so I quit listening.

He didn't go to work the next day. That meant a lot of trouble for his foreman and no money for us.

 There was a time when he was responsible for a large project. I visited a shrine many times to pray for his success.

Oh, I wish my wife could hear that.

 Because of my sincere prayers, everything went very well, but he never gave me one word of thanks.

 The family next door to us takes nice trips to hot-spring resorts.

We never have, not even once!

 But, I heard that lately you and wives in the neighborhood went on a trip together.

 Yeah well, I need to get away once in a while. And I had to use my rainy-day savings to go!

As the kids grow up, they need clothes and money for school. When I tell my husband, he ignores me.

I pack him the same lunch I make for our growing kids, but he gripes that he doesn't like it.

That's why I can't send him off to work with a smile. I feel badly about that.

So I wait for the chance to say I'm sorry about what happened, but he stays out late and comes home drunk.

Then he demands more to drink. Who would give him more? Not me!

You poured your heart out, didn't you?

Forgive me, but the more I talk, the madder I get. I can't stop talking.

She's just as tough as Mr. Kuma.

Don't embarrass me...

Now I know your circumstances and understand the cause of your suffering.

You've been putting up with it a long time, haven't you?

Well, what can you do with such a husband?

Grandpa, please cure his drinking problem.

I said I knew the cause of the problem, but I didn't say I could do something about it.

What do you mean?

Actually, I am sorry to say that the person who needs to do something is you, Mrs. Kuma.

What!? Me?

Yes, the cause of your suffering is your own behavior, Mrs. Kuma.

Huh?!?..

Mr. Kuma is not the cause, she is? What a surprise! They say Truth (Nobody says "comedy is stranger than fiction")

All of a sudden this story has an unexpected twist to it.

Hachi seems bewildered, but Grandpa's words are true.

The story of the Truth of Cause is approaching the climax, and they are going to make a further investigation into the cause of suffering.

This is such an important process that we will talk about it in greater detail next time.

That's all for now, ladies and gentlemen. Thank you very much.

The Truh that Rids Suffering, Gives Hope, and Unleashes Courage (Four Noble Truths) Truth of Cause 2
Ten Suchnesses

The wife came to see Grandpa

because she wanted to change her husband who drinks too much and does not go to work. Right?

Hachi thought Grandpa was going to give Mr. Kuma a good talking to...

However, Grandpa said it was the wife, not Mr. Kuma, who needed to make a change.

He surprised both Hachi and Mrs. Kuma.

This time, let's see how Grandpa explains what he means according to the teaching of the Ten Suchnesses.

Grandpa, are you saying that I am wrong,

not my husband who drinks and doesn't go to work?

Yeah, I feel pretty sorry for Mrs. Kuma.

Well, well. I might have surprised you, but listen.

Are you familiar with the Ten Suchnesses?

No, I never heard of them.

The Ten Suchnesses tell us that everything in this world exists because of appearance, nature, substance, potency,

function, cause, condition, effect, recompense, and – from beginning to the end – an ultimate integration of them all.

I don't know about appearance, nature, and substance, but I've heard about causes and conditions.

We heard about them when you taught the Dharma of Causation.

Yes, yes ....

Everything has a cause, and when it comes into contact with a condition, they produce an effect. Isn't that so?

However, if you want to eliminate your suffering, you must look closely at the specific reason.

What do you mean by "appearance, nature, and substance..."?

I will explain the meaning of each one before I talk about your suffering.

Appearance

Nature

Substance

Potency

Function

Cause

Condition

Effect

Recompense

Ultimate Integration of Them All

The list looks like this:

Hmm, do you understand, Mrs. Kuma?

Only as well as you do, Hachi...

Could you explain them a little more?

Appearance
Nature
Substance
Potency
Function
Cause
Condition
Effect – result
Recompense
Ultimate Integral

In fact, every existing thing has a certain appearance; such an appearance has an appropriate nature; such a nature has a substance;

such substance has potency; such potency has a function - always directed outwardly.

In this world, all things are interconnected and they give rise to phenomena. It all starts with a cause.

But causes don't create effects unless they meet with various conditions.

So if the cause meets the condition, and they produce an effect, then this effect will have an influence. This is called "recompense."

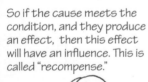

These nine elements are continually in a complex knot,

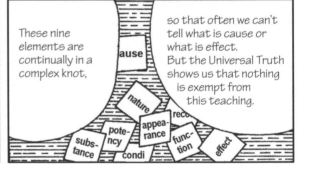

so that often we can't tell what is cause or what is effect. But the Universal Truth shows us that nothing is exempt from this teaching.

In other words, from appearance to recompense, from beginning to end, everything is integrated in this teaching.

Grandpa, what a good explanation. Do you understand?

About as well as you do, Hachi...

Could you please explain in simple words?

You two are funny - asking me to explain in more detail or in a simpler way.

An attitude and behavior that is part of your nature is a cause- when that cause comes into contact with a condition- they produce an effect.

More simply?

Nature and condition produce an effect.

Good! Good! Good!

You sound like a cheerleader.

Sorry, I'm still not getting it yet.

Okay, in a word, everything is a manifestation of your mind.

Excuse me, but does that have anything to do with my husband's drinking?

I said "it applies to everything," so of course it does.

How?

Let's review your story.

My husband said that he wanted to do a good job, but his foreman pressured him to finish early and save money.

And I got tired of hearing him complain about the same thing.

65

Because of my hundreds of visits to the shrine, the gods blessed my husband's work.

But, my husband never thanked me.

Our neighbors go to hot-spring resorts, but not us. I need money for our kids, but he ignores me.

There are other things, too!

Oh, I talk too much.

By the way, I want to ask you, what do you think of your husband's work?

Of course, I think his work is important because he supports our family with it.

So, you don't care what kind of work he does as long as he brings money home. Isn't that right?

Sure, as long as he isn't doing anything illegal.

Well then, I am going to ask you, Hachi - you've been a landscaper for a long time. Do you think you could be a carpenter?

Hah?! Well, I mean, I suppose I could but I'd need a lot of training...

OK. So would you start training to become a carpenter tomorrow if you were promised more money?

Humm, no, I wouldn't because I like my work as a landscaper...

If I asked Mr. Kuma the same thing, what would he answer?

He is so proud of being a carpenter, I can't imagine him agreeing to do anything else.

What do you think, Mrs.Kuma?

I never realized he was so proud of his profession.

He takes pride in his work. Isn't that why he was frustrated with the way his foreman ran the business?

Yes, that's right.

And how did you treat him?

I didn't think about his feelings at all.

Your husband might be a little self-centered, but I have to say, so are you.

This is what I meant a little while ago when I said that every phenomenon is a manifestation of your mind.

In other words, the effect that is produced depends on your nature, and the effect can appear to be completely different if you change your attitude. This is what the Ten Suchnesses teaches us.

That is why Grandpa said that the cause of Mrs. Kuma's suffering is inside her.

Right. Instead of trying to change Mr. Kuma, if Mrs. Kuma changes her attitude and behavior, Mr. Kuma will change, too.

Grandpa told us that Mrs. Kuma's current problem stems from her complaining about her husband.

Grandpa's story is full of meaning, isn't it?

You can't hear such a meaningful story from a comic. I don't know how much Mrs. Kuma understood.

Four Noble Truths
(Truth of Cause; Ten Suchnesses)

Next we will look into the world of her mind by studying the Ten Realms and Three Thousand Worlds in One Thought.

The Truh that Rids Suffering, Gives Hope, and Unleashes Courage (Four Noble Truths) Truth of Cause 3

The Ten Realms of Being Found in One Another

Four Noble Truths (The Ten Realms and Three Thousand Worlds in One Thought)

In the previous chapter, we learned the Truth of Cause.

The wife's attitude and behavior are the cause of her current unhappy state.

If she changes herself, Mr. Kuma will also change.

Hachi and Mrs. Kuma agreed with Grandpa's analysis,

but does that mean they truly understood?

That is why Grandpa decided to teach the Ten Realms of Being Found in One Another.

And he suggested Mrs. Kuma to see the realms of her own mind.

Grandpa's home

There is a teaching called the Ten Realms of Being Found in One Another.

Yes?

Are you familiar with it?

No, I've never heard of it before.

Well, you were so quick to reply earlier that I thought you knew all about it.

Sorry, I was just pretending.

There are ten different realms in one's mind.

That is wonderful!

Wonderful? What do you mean?

Aren't realms the same as worlds, like Disney World?

Disney World wasn't around in my day. Anyway, it's not exactly wonderful.

Why not?

Grandpa, don't make such a face. Just tell us about the Ten Realms.

Within the Ten Realms, there are Four Realms of Sages: (1) Shravaka, one who listens to the teachings; (2) Pratyekabuddha, one wanting to reach enlightenment by personally practicing the teachings;

(3) Bodhisattva, one who helps others and themselves to reach enlightenment; (4) Buddha, an awakened one living for humanity.

Wow, so many difficult realms.

Yes, they are difficult but if you want badly enough to reach them, you can.

What are the other six?

The Six Realms are:

The Realm of Hell (anger)

The
Realm of
Hungry
Spirits
(greed)

The
Realm of
Animals
(ignorance)

The
Realm of
Demons
(aggression)

72

The Realm of Human Beings (normal state)

The State of Hell

The State of Demons

The State of Beasts

The Realm of Heaven (joy)

We are always moving in and out of the Six Realms. This is called transmigration within the Six Realms.

That sounds awful.

Do those realms exist in the mind?

Of course, And they exist in your mind, too.

In my mind, too?

Yes. Think about it for a minute.

...

He drinks a lot and doesn't go to work.

I want to buy things. I need money, but he doesn't give me any.

He owes a lot of his success to my sincere prayers at the shrine, but he never acknowledges that.

He doesn't work much lately. He just gets drunk. He finds money for drinks, but not for me.

I know I should not be such a complainer, but I can't help it.

I want to go to the a hot-spring resort once in a while to relax.

By the way, do you recognize some of the Six Realms in what you've said?

Oh, yes.

What you have described just now are the Six Realms.

Really?

What a terrible attitude I have!

Well, don't be too disappointed.

In the beginning, I explained the Four Realms of the Sages; but sages also have the Six Realms of Being just like us.

And ordinary people also have the Four Realms of the Sages.

We live in the Ten Realms with ten different minds.

Well, that means …

Ordinary people can reach the Sage Realms by being compassionate. Don't you sometimes sincerely worry about your husband's health because of his drinking? That caring is the same as the Buddha's compassionate heart.

I'm glad to hear that.

But we repeatedly move in and out of these Six Realms.

I wouldn't get so mad if he worked hard and stopped drinking.

Don't look outside yourself – look inside. The cause of your suffering is your focus on yourself. There is an expression: "The triple world of desire, form, and formlessness is a manifestation of the mind alone."

Then, are you saying that my mind is creating the world I am in now?

75

That's right! If you change your attitude and behavior, Mr. Kuma will change accordingly.

This is called, Three Thousand Worlds in One Thought. A single thought decides three thousand worlds.

What should I do?

Try to reflect on all this, take a good inventory of your thoughts and put yourself in his shoes.

Yes ....

But just reflecting is not enough. You need to apply what you learn and make it a practice. Otherwise, the result will never change.

I understand. I am going to change my attitude and practice the teachings.

That's good! I feel better.

Four Noble Truths
(The Ten Realms and Three Thousand Worlds in One Thought)

Well, she seems to have understood.

This is the end of learning the Truth of Cause.

Four Noble Truths
(The Ten Realms and Three Thousand Worlds in One Thought)

Next time we will see how Mr. Kuma responds to his wife's change (Truth of Path)

and how his response will affect people around him.

The Truh that Rids Suffering, Gives Hope, and Unleashes Courage (Four Noble Truths)
Truth of Path and Truth of Extinction

Four Noble Truths
(The Truth of Path and the Truth of Extinction)

We studied the Truth of the Cause of Suffering and learned that our suffering is the result of our attitude and behavior.

However, just knowing this is not enough.

What we understand has to be manifest in your behavior and attitude. Learning is nothing without practice.

The Truth of Path means living the teachings.

If we do so, we will gain true happiness as a result. That is called the Truth of Extinction.

Let's listen to Grandpa. He will show how to use the teachings in our daily lives.

From now on, I will try to change my attitude and behavior.

What will you do when you go home?

Well, I am going to change myself . . . and then I'll start feeling better!

How?

I will try to understand how my husband feels by having a drink myself.

Just kidding.

Clearly, there's no easy answer when Grandpa asks what you are actually going to do . . .

Well then, let me explain the teachings of Right View and Donation.

"The View" and "The Nation?" Aren't those talk shows?

I will get mad if you say that you saw them on TV.

Ahh, I must be mistaken.

Right View, means that you see things in line with the Truth (Dharma)

Right View

Try not to see your husband with your self-centered mind.

Then what kind of view is better?

Don't look for his shortcomings, look for his good points. For example, he wants to do good work.

Yes, he has that good quality.

I agree. Next, I want to talk about donation. Donation can mean putting yourself in somebody else's shoes, and living by being more aware.

You mean that I should let him do whatever he wants to do?

No, just try to understand WHY he wants to do it.

For example, take him seriously. What he's saying aren't just complaints.

Listen as if your roles were reversed. That is one meaning of Donation.

When Mr. Kuma comes home from work, welcome him with kind words and a smile. This is your practice of donation.

That's easy—

"Welcome home!"

You say it's easy, but you have been angry at him.

You're right.

I understand how self-centered I was.

Glad you realized that. You are a smart person. You can handle the situation, can't you?

I will apologize to him when I get home.

I learned a lot, too!

Please do your best!

Caw!

Caw!

Mr. Kuma did not go to work.

Dinner is ready, honey.

Already?

You made a feast today – all of my favorites...

Yes, as a matter of fact, I want to apologize to you.

What?

You didn't damage my tools, did you?

No, I went to see Grandpa today.

What happened?

I learned the Four Noble Truths. It made me realize that I've been self-centered.

I didn't understand your strong desire to do good work, no matter what your foreman told you. Please forgive me.

You're not the only one to blame. I, too...

...

Are you going out to drink?

I need to go out. I'll be right back.

Where did he go? Did he go out to drink?

I'm home.

Welcome home. You're back early. Did you go out for a drink?

No, I realized that I had been self-centered.

I've always complained about my boss, but I never thought of his side of the situation.

When I realized that, I couldn't help but go and apologize to him.

At first he wasn't very receptive, but as he listened, he began to understand what I had to say.

To my surprise, my boss apologized for being so demanding.

I am so glad to hear that.

I am going to work tomorrow.

It's just like what Grandpa said; If I change, my world changes.

The wife understood logically what Grandpa taught her, but when she actually applied what she'd learned and saw the results,

the Buddha's teaching became her own.

Her happiness or unhappiness depends on her attitude and her behavior.

Next time, I will introduce you to the Dharma of Twelve Causes and Conditions, which teaches us the workings of the mind.

Four Noble Truths
(The Truth of the Path and the Truth of Extinction)

The Truh that Rids Suffering, Gives Hope, and Unleashes Courage (Four Noble Truths) Truth of Cause 4
The Dharma of Twelve Causes and Conditions

Four Noble Truths
(Dharma of Twelve Causes and Conditions)

Thank you for listening to me again. Last time, we finished the Four Noble Truths by learning the

Truth of Path and the Truth of Extinction.

Four Noble Truths
(Dharma of Twelve Causes and Conditions)

This time, let's learn the Dharma of Twelve Causes and Conditions as another way to find the Cause of Suffering.

How are you, Grandpa? I am sorry to bother you.

What's the problem, Hachi?

To tell you the truth, a friend of mine is suffering because her husband drinks too much, just like Mr. Kuma.

He doesn't go to work, either?

Not exactly, but I'd like to help her solve the problem by applying the teaching of the Four Noble Truths.

That's kind of you, but will you listen to me before you try to help her?

OK...

I used the teaching of the Ten Suchnesses so that Mrs. Kuma could find out what caused her suffering. But there is another teaching, The Dharma of Twelve Causes and Conditions.

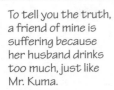

The Dharma of Twelve Causes and Conditions?

Yes. As you learned, everything in this world changes constantly, but the changes come from one universal Dharma. That Dharma consists of twelve parts.

That sounds like the Dharma of Cause and Effect.

Good guess - that's what it is.

That's good.

The Dharma of Twelve Causes and Conditions shows both the outer causation (physical growth) and the inner causation (mental growth). They explain our growth in twelve phases.

Physical growth and mental growth?

It teaches how human beings are formed, grow old, and die in three periods – the past, present, and future – both physically and mentally. It also teaches us the essential way to purify our minds and extinguish illusions.

Can you explain it in simple terms?

OK, let's talk about the "inner" causation, before I get into your friend's problem.

The Dharma of Twelve Causes and Conditions

1. **Illusion (ignorance)** — Not knowing the "right view" of the world and life

2. **Action** — Habitual activity

3. **Consciousness** — Recognizing habits

4. **Name and Form** — Mental function and the physical body

5. **Six Entrances of Sensation** — The eyes, ears, nose, tongue, skin, and mind (related to the senses)

6. **Contact** — Recognition and decision

7. **Feelings** — Affection, feelings of suffering, joy, and likes or dislikes

8. **Desire** — Attachment

9. **Clinging** — Choices

10. **Existence** — Discrimination

11. **Birth** — Suffering begins

12. **Old Age and Death** — All types of suffering

A chart of the 12 Links, would look like this...

Please explain a bit more.

Let's apply it to your friend's problem.

Her husband drinks too much, doesn't he?

Yes, I also know that her father drank a lot and was abusive to her mother. She's had a hard life because of him.

That is very sad.

So she has been holding a grudge against her father.

I see.

That's why she married a man who didn't drink. She did not want to go through the same thing as her mother.

After they got married, her husband started drinking?

That's right.

Her suffering stems from her dislike of his drinking, doesn't it?

Yes, she has a bad feeling about drinking.

In that case, she has a serious hatred toward drinkers. Is that right?

Yes, that was why she wanted to marry a non-drinker.

She feels that way unconsciously about everyone who drinks?

I guess so.

She has developed a habit of hating her father and has a prejudice against all drinkers.

By the way, what caused her father to drink?

I don't know, but I heard that he owned a successful business. It later failed and he went bankrupt.

After that, he started to drink a lot. He died at a young age.

After his business failed, he couldn't help drinking, I guess.

Your friend has resented her father for a long time, but I wonder if she has ever thought of her father's feelings - what drove him to drink.

I guess not.

Has she always thought of her father as irresponsible?

Yes, she has.

But she hated her father being irresponsible, and she probably has convinced herself that all drinkers are irresponsible.

I should say that the root cause of her suffering was not being able to see anything from his perspective – to understand why he drank.

That is exactly right.

According to "Inner causation," your friend began to hate her father simply by judging what he did without being sensitive to his feelings. She became totally negative to any drinking. And that led to hatred toward everyone who drinks.

Hachi, talk to her and tell her that it must have been very hard for her. Try to help her see the reality of her self-pity. Help her to become compassionate and see how her father really felt. If she understands her father, she can have a memorial service for him. That is the best thing she can do.

Yes, I will talk to her.

When she reflects and is able to shift her perspective about her father, her way of looking at her husband will also change. Her suffering will be gone.

If she sees her husband differently, she will be able to serve him and enjoy spending time with him.

Thank you very much.

Four Noble Truths
(Dharma of Twelve Causes and Conditions)

Thanks to Grandpa's advice, Hachi understood that the way to find the primary cause of suffering depends upon the origin of the problem.

Four Noble Truths
(Dharma of Twelve Causes and Conditions)

We have finished studying the Four Noble Truths. Next time, let's review them.

The teaching that resolves suffering in our life, giving us hope and courage (Four Noble Truths)

The Four Noble Truths (Conclusion)

Four Noble Truths (Conclusion)

We have been learning the Four Noble Truths in six series.

Now we will review them, and see the sequel to the story.

I see you're home, Grandpa?

Oh, how are things going?

Well...

What's the matter? You look gloomy today.

Well, it's not my problem, but it's my friend's.

Oh, the lady who was suffering because of her husband's drinking?

Yes, Grandpa, I told her about the Four Noble Truths that you explained to Mrs. Kuma.

That's great! How did you tell her?

First, I told her that the Four Noble Truths are a way to free herself from suffering.

There's the Truth of Suffering—Cause, Path, and Extinction.

The Truth of Suffering, teaches us to squarely face our suffering.

The Truth of Cause, teaches us to search for the cause of the suffering.

The Truth of Path, teaches us to walk the right path in life by practicing the Dharma.

If we do this we will be free from suffering and lead a happy life.

That's what I said.

Did she understand?

Yes, she told me that she understood and went home happy.

Did she get good results?

Well, I visited her the other day to see how she was doing, but she didn't look pleased.

Is that so?

I asked her how things were at home.

She thought she understood the Four Noble Truths, but she could not apply them to her daily life, right?

Wow! Grandpa did you already know that family's situation?

No, but that's a common story.

What?

It's because we are all creatures of habit.

Habits?

Yes, that is called "karma" in Buddhism.

What is karma?

Karma can mean habitual action. There are positive actions as well as negative actions.

Through her habits, she has become habitually attached to poor choices.

So, although she understands the teaching intellectually, It is very hard for her to change her habits.

You mean there's nothing she can do?

No, she can break her habit of making poor choices through deep self-reflection.

Does self-reflection mean admitting our mistakes?

Yes, but when we have had a self-centered attitude for such a long time, we have difficulty solving our problems even though we can understand the solution. We need to apply the teaching of the Truth of Path.

You're right! She understood what I said, but didn't reflect on her resentment toward her father.

That's it. Next time lead the person to self-reflection.

Oh, I understand. Now I have mastered the Four Noble Truths.

Well, well, well …

What do you mean by that?

You shouldn't think the Four Noble Truths only teach you how to solve your problems.

You mean they do more than just solve our problems?

Yes, they also teach us a practical order for our thought processes.

…

Let's take your job as and example.

Landscaping?

Yes. When do you get your orders?

Usually, when plants or trees are overgrown.

When you come to the garden, what do you do first?

I take a good look around to find the places in the garden that need the most care.

Then I start working until it is all done.

Doesn't that same process apply to the practice of the Four Noble Truths?

My work is just like the Four Noble Truths?

You look into the disarray of the garden (the Truth of Suffering). You search for the cause (the Truth of Cause). Then you work diligently to repair the garden (the Truth of Path). Then the garden becomes beautiful (the Truth of Extinction).

Indeed! That sounds so easy!

You say so, but if you don't notice the disarray in the garden, what will happen?

Or if you start cutting trees without thinking or planning, what is the result?

If you don't approach the work in the right way, what will happen?

Each part of the process is essential to have a beautiful garden.

In other words, without constant practice, even simple things get out of control.

The teaching of the Four Noble Truths is not just a problem-solving tool, it is also a foundation for thinking and acting. I really understand it this time.

How are you, Grandpa?

Oh, hello. Now everybody is here.

Thanks to you, things are back to normal.

Now I get along with my boss.

At first, when Grandpa told me I was wrong, I resented it.

In my mind, I thought my husband was wrong. That's why I resisted apologizing to him.

But, I reflected and saw my shortcomings and did as you suggested.

Yes, it is hard to do, but the Buddha's teachings help us have a happier life.

Now, my suffering seems like it was only a bad dream…

Your present happiness comes from this suffering. Without the suffering you would never know the Dharma.

So, suffering is an opportunity to learn the meaning of happiness?

Great! You've got it!

From now on, all of you can be a good example and teach the Dharma to those who are suffering.

We'll do our best!

It seems like they will all spread the Buddha's teachings – wonderful!

This completes the Four Noble Truths.

Thank you. Another story is coming up.

The Eight Precepts for Spiritual Growth (The Eightfold Path)
Right View, Right Thought

It consists of: *Right View, Right Thought, Right Speech Right Action, Right Living Right Effort, Right Mindfulness, Right Concentration* "Right" means being in agreement with Universal Truth (Dharma), or in harmony with others.

(Praying) Please bless us this year.

(Praying) Please bless us this year.

It is good weather for a New Year's visit to the shrine.

Yes, I feel great.

Let's go out to eat.

Well, how about noodles?

No, I want to eat a big steak.

That's too expensive.

Don't be stingy.

Are you saying I'm stingy?

You said I'm extravagant.

Hello, you two...

What? Can't you see we're busy!

Yes, I know. I was listening to you.

How embarrassing.

I think I might be able to help you.

Mind your own business!

Don't be mad.

By the way, do you see those smokestacks over there? How many are there?

102

That's called a "phantom smokestack."

Depending on where you're standing, they line up with each other, don't they?

When I saw them from over here, they looked different.

Just now, you two reminded me of those smokestacks.

What do you mean?

Well, your husband thinks that you see one,

and you think he sees two.

What are you talking about?

There is a teaching called the Eightfold Path in Buddhism.

Sorry, we can't stay...

Wait... this is for your own happiness.

Make it quick.

The beginning of the Eightfold Path is: Right View and Right Thought.

Right View and Right Thought?

Yes. Here's a question-

What is this, a game show?

A while ago, you said that your husband was a big spender, didn't you?

Yes, we're newlyweds and don't have much money.

And didn't you say that your wife was stingy?

Yes, she has been so thrifty. I thought we could celebrate a bit for New Year's.

Why do you want to be thrifty?

Because my husband works so hard, I don't want to waste any money.

Did you hear her? Do you still want to be extravagant?

No, I know that she has been very careful about spending money,

which was why I wanted to treat her for New Year's

Do you see what was happening?

. . . .

You two were arguing because of your concern for each other!

You're right!

On the surface, it looked like two different perspectives. But in reality there is a third perspective, which is both of you being considerate of each other.

We were thinking of each other, but we didn't realize it.

That's right. If you saw things from the other person's perspective, and not from your self-centered view, you wouldn't have argued.

Oh, that's Right View?

Yes. And Right Thought means that you leave behind your narrow, selfish thoughts, take a broad view of the situation, and think about it correctly.

In other words, you eliminate greed, anger, and ill will from your thinking.

Yes. I got mad because she didn't like my idea.

But I was selfish, too.

I'm glad you understand.

In Right View and Right Thought, what does "right" mean?

"Right" means that something is in agreement with Universal Truth (Dharma), and is harmonious and appropriate to the situation.

What you say is kind of vague...

You're very critical, aren't you?

Don't take it personally, that's just my nature.

"Right" means not being misled by ego or preconceived ideas.

Thanks to your good advice, our year is off to a good start!

Yes, I'm glad to be able to see things from my husband's point of view.

I am glad to help you.

I'll be appearing in the next chapter, so don't forget me!

I'm sorry that I started the New Year by arguing with you.

Me, too.

Let's ask for a blessing one more time.

OK

Please bless us this year, too.

Please bless us this year, too.

I feel better.

Do you remember the first time we prayed, "Please bless us this year" but the second time we prayed "Please bless us this year as well"?

Actually, the first time I prayed, "Please bless me with happiness this year."

Oh, so did I . .

I realized that I was happy to have a good wife whom I care about and who cares about me, too.

That is why you prayed "... again this year."

I hope that we will continue to be happy so that we can say "... again this year" next New Year.

The Eight Precepts for Spiritual Growth (The Eightfold Path)
Right Speech, Right Action

This time we will learn: Right Speech (No lying, being two-faced, slandering, or improper language), Right Action (your daily conduct follows the Buddha's Path).

Where's the best place?

Should I go over there?

What are we going to do if one of us catches more than the other?

Let's put all of our beans together and divide them in two.

OK, Let's do our best.

"Out with the bad"

"In with the good"

I got a lot!

Look at how much I've got.

Me, too!

Let's put them all together.

Are we going to divide them in two?

Yeah.

In fact, both pretended to put them all together, but both hid some in their pockets.

Hello!

How are you!

Hey, he's talking to a dog.

That's weird...

Did you say something?

You think I'm a strange monk, don't you?

We didn't say anything...well, goodbye.

Wait, you don't have to be afraid of me.

I've never seen anyone talk to a dog.

Do you talk to people?

Yeah.

So you talk to human beings but not to other living beings?

It's not normal.

The Buddha teaches us that all existence has "buddha-nature."

We gotta go study now—

If you just stay for three minutes, I will teach you an important life lesson that you won't find in any textbook.

Just 3 minutes, OK?

OK! There is a teaching called the Eightfold Path in Buddhism. Right Speech and Right Action are part of that path.

What does that have to do with talking to a dog?

It has to do with "Right Action."

What is Right Action?

Right Action means: no killing, stealing, or gambling.

Hey! We're just kids…

Oh, I am sorry. It also means that you should not be wasteful, or make trouble.

This may seem obvious, but it may make you realize something.

Also, it means having good manners. For example, in your everyday life,

when someone asks you to do something, you should answer them cheerfully. You should greet people politely and clean up after yourself.

But we're already doing those things.

Really?

Do you remember what I said about every existence having buddha-nature?

You mean when you were talking to the dog?

Buddhism teaches you to not only respect human beings, but revere the buddha-nature of every living thing, too.

Revering someone's buddha-nature?

In short, we should respect and appreciate everybody and everything –

not only living things, but also mountains, rivers, and trees.

Really.

I happened to see a dog, so I greeted him.

You talk to everybody and everything? Wow! You must be very busy.

A mind that respects every encounter is far more important than how the outward action may appear.

Then why did you talk to the dog?

I wanted to get your attention.

No wonder I thought it was strange.

We already have a home altar. We need to get going now...

Wait, I still have a few minutes left.

But ...

I want to tell you about Right Speech.

What's that?

It means you should speak in the right way.

Aren't we doing that?

You are, but how about the Four Evils of Speech?

The Four Evils of Speech?

Yes. They are telling lies, being insincere, speaking ill of others, and careless speech.

Wow!

The boys were reminded of the beans they hid in their pockets.

You may speak politely, but if what you say isn't right, then it's no good.

Words have the power to deepen your friendship and trust, or destroy your relationship.

That's why our words need to show gratitude, respect, and consideration for the person we're talking to.

Thank you very much for the great lesson, sir.

You appreciate me - that makes me feel great. That is Right Speech.

Oh, my three minutes are up! Goodbye.

It just dawned on me, I think I still have some candy in my pocket.

Me, too! Let's count them again.

The numbers weren't very different from the first count, but their hearts were warm as spring sunshine.

The Eight Precepts for Spiritual Growth (The Eightfold Path)

Right Living, Right Effort, Right Mindfulness, Right Concentration

We are going to learn Right Living (making an honest living and living within one's means), Right Effort (right conduct in living), Right Mindfulness (maintaining right frame of mind toward oneself and others), and Right Concentration (striving constantly for the true Dharma without being distracted by any change of circumstances).

Thank you for coming to pray for the memorial service.

Thanks especially to the young ones.

The young ones remind me of my childhood. I was a novice at the temple. Something happened back then that is related to Right Livelihood,

Right Effort, Right Mindfulness, and Right Concentration from the Eightfold Path.

I'd like to tell you that story. Two young men were earnestly praying.

Please help me get accepted at my university.

Please help me get accepted at my university.

118

This is great – we prayed at the best temple.

Oh no! Someone else offered the same prayer as I did.

What the..?! someone else offered the same prayer as I did.

The competition also made their wish at this temple - that will ruin my chances!

Let's take them down.

whoosh

Uh, oh!

Oh no! That novice saw us.

Hey, what are you looking at?

What did you pray for?

Us?

We came here to pray to get into university.

Why do you want to get into university?

I want to enter the Economics Department.

When I graduate, I can get into a good company and become a manager or executive. I might be able to marry my boss's daughter.

That marriage might be a good foothold for my success.

Wouldn't that be great?

Oh
...

And how about you?

I want to get into medical school.

After graduation, I can work for a big hospital.

I will try to become head physician and then open my own hospital.

Doctors make a lot of money,

you know.

Well, as for me, I heard about the Eightfold Path from my master.

What is that?

Will it help us get into a good school?

The EightFold Path consists of Right View, Right Thought, Right Speech, Right Action, Right Living, Right Effort, Right Mindfulness and Right Concentration.

That sounds difficult –

What kind of mantra is that?

It's not a mantra; it's a teaching about the right way of living, taught by Shakyamuni Buddha.

So, see things in the right way, and think in the right way.

Talk in the right way and act in the right way.

What is the next thing, Right Living?

It means to live in the right way.

Right Living?

Right Effort means diligently practicing right conduct in everyday life. Right Mindfulness is to have right thoughts for yourself and others.

We are making the right effort, at least where we are concerned.

"Right" means not only for you, but also for others. So make an effort to be happy yourself and make others happy, too.

My effort isn't enough?

Why did you suddenly decide to tell us about the Eightfold Path?

Well...

Something about you two reminded me of that teaching.

Are you saying that we are doing something wrong?

You say "right" or "wrong," but they change according to the time and place, don't they?

Yeah! We are aiming to become an entrepreneur and a doctor. What's wrong with that?

Medicine is a noble profession.

I don't have a great deal of knowledge, but isn't a doctor one who takes care of the sick?

Yeah, in the olden days they said, "medicine is the art of kindness."

Well my uncle was a doctor, and he was arrested for tax evasion. He always looked angry - his face was far from kind.

122

He was more interested in money.

I heard that his son was going to a village without a doctor.

You know if he goes there, he won't have any chance to move up and he won't make very much money.

But he looks full of life!

I believe he's happy because he chose to help people in need. That is Right Living.

Aha …

I understood Right Mindfulness, but what about the other one?

Right Concentration?

What does that mean?

Don't waver - always living the right way.

What do you mean by "waver"?

In life, we encounter many temptations, but we should not be wavering. Keep a steady mind.

We read about corruption in the business world a lot. That's the opposite from Right Living, huh?

I'm disappointed when I see important people doing bad things.

They could be a good example of "Right Living."

"Gong" "Gong"

Oh, my teacher is calling, I have to go.

He made me think...

We treated him like a kid, but he taught us a lot!

Yeah, I'm glad he told us what he's learned. That was worth listening to...

The Eightfold Path is a daily way to Right Living.

Let's put these two wishes back where they were...

These two students seemed to realize the importance of Right Living, Right Effort, Right Mindfulness, and Right Concentration.

I sincerely hope all of you learned the Eightfold Path,

and can put it into practice every day.

Six Paramitas That Lead to Spiritually Rich Living (Six Practices)

Donation 1

The Six Paramitas (donation, precept-keeping, forbearance, effort, meditation, and wisdom) are bodhisattva practices that lead us to attain enlightenment. They are six standards that guide us in service to others and society. This time we will learn Donation – donating material goods, the Dharma (Buddha's Teachings), and physical donation (volunteering).

Last time, we learned the Eightfold Path - the path of practices to put your conduct in order and be free from distractions.

This time we learn the Six Paramitas. These are the bodhisattva's six virtues.

In other words, they show the Bodhisattva Path,

which is devoting ourselves to serving other people and our world. They are: Donation, Precept-keeping, Patience, Diligence, Meditation, and Wisdom.

I know, I see "patients" at the hospital all the time.

You need to get back on your medicine...

No, not that meaning of "patients."

Hmmm…

It's about bodhisattvas.

Oh, bodhisattvas – I have a feeling that I'd heard about them somewhere.

It's about the Bodhisattva Manjushri and the Bodhisattva Maitreya.

You know them pretty well?

Of course. I studied Buddhism. Bodhisattvas are very important.

Yes, Manjushri and Maitreya are important! But I want to tell you about the bodhisattvas closer to you.

Bodhisattvas closer to me?

Yes, you have the ability to become a bodhisattva.

I can become a bodhisattva?

Yes, anyone who practices the Six Paramitas with a desire to help others.

What are you saying? An ignorant old woman like her can become a bodhisattva?

Yes, if she diligently practices the Six Paramitas

I can't understand if it's too complicated ...

I'll make it easy for you.

The first step of the Six Paramitas is Donation. It means giving, right?

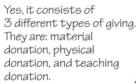
Yes, it consists of 3 different types of giving. They are: material donation, physical donation, and teaching donation.

How about some examples?

Material donation means to give money and things to others in need. Physical donation means taking action to remove someone's worries or burden. Teaching donation can be anything - for example, to help others learn the Dharma, and spread the wisdom of the Lotus Sutra.

I don't have any money to give…

You've been teaching young women how to cook. That is a teaching donation.

I don't even have a talent like that.

I saw you cleaning the streets and the temple grounds. That is a physical donation.

That's bodhisattva practice? We were practicing donation without knowing it!

But the simplest practice is to give money, isn't it?

That is important, too.

I put a lot of money in a donation box the other day to make a wish come true.

Oh!

The more money you donate, the better return, right?

Oh!

I am thinking about donating a lot so that I will make a good profit.

Well ...

What happened? Why do you look so serious?

I'd like to tell you a famous story.

1,500 years ago in India there was a monk named Bodhidharma.

Bodhidharma went to China.

In those days, China was divided into 2 empires - Northern Wei and Liang.

The first emperor of Liang was called Emperor Wu.

He was a devout Buddhist. At age 63, he began the practice of *shashin*.

Shashin means to donate all of your wealth to a temple and donate yourself to being the custodian of the temple.

Shortly after he started that practice, Bodhidharma came to China and met him.

He proudly put a question to Bodhidharma.

I built a temple, trained monks, copied a sutra, and made a statue of the Buddha.

I did such great things, what kind of wonderful merit do you think I will receive?

No merit.

What?

No merit!

Why was that?

I can see two different ways of thinking.

First, if you do things only because you want merit, it is not the right kind of donation.

What?

Second, you can do good things like that emperor - just "doing," is already a great merit.

You mean to make a donation just for the sake of donating, no strings attached? So that's it?

No, it means that the moment that you make a donation, your "greedy" mind disappears. That is great merit.

The emperor was probably surprised to hear what Bodhidharma told him, but he must have understood.

What makes you think so?

Because, he did *shashin* three times before he died at 85.

Now I understand the meaning of the "merit of donation." Thank you very much.

By the way, there are other kinds of donation - for example, the Seven Generosities of the Poor.

I will tell you about that next time.

Six Paramitas That Lead to Spiritually Rich Living (Six Practices)

Donation 2

We are going to learn Donation (Seven Generocities of the Poor), which is Donation of the Eyes, Donation of Smile, Donation of Speech, Physical Donation (Donation of good deeds for other people), Mental Donation, Giving Up Your Seat to Others, and Finding Shelter for the Needy.

Last time, we talked about Donation in the Six Paramitas.

Material donation, physical donation, and teaching donation.

Are there other kinds of generosities?

Yes, I will talk about the Seven Generosities of the Poor.

What are they?

They are donations that the poor and the sick can give.

That suits me. I have lots of time, but no money.

Young man, you seem too busy to do anything, but you have money, right?

Yeah, but I want to hear about the Seven Generosities of the Poor.

Young man, you seemed to have changed since you heard about deeds without receiving anything in return. Now you are stingy.

No, I am curious about the Seven Generosities.

That is wonderful.

Please tell us.

First is the Donation of the Eyes.

I should give my eye?

No, no. Nothing that extreme. It means to look at people kindly.

I see.

Next, is to greet people with a smile.

I see, I see.

Third, is to speak softly to people.

Fourth, is to do good deeds for other people.

You told us about that donation before.

But I am not that strong.

Hard work is not the only physical donation.

Putting palms together in reverence – revering the buddha-nature in others – and being courteous, are also great generosities.

Well I can 'do that.

I am truly moved.

You look like you are moved.

Yes, my way of living is well suited to the Seven Generosities of the Poor.

Oh, that is wonderful.

In what way?

I see people I don't like at work.

I can look at them kindly.

Oh, that's Donation of the Eyes.

I force myself to smile and I flatter my customers by saying,

"I know how you feel."

pretending as if I really understood their feelings.

 Do you call that Donation of Speech?

 Finally, I act like I'm working hard for them.

 Is that what you call Physical Donation?

 Don't you think I'm following the teachings of Donation?

 Well ...

 What are you thinking now?

 Let me tell you a very famous story.

 Over 100 years ago, at the White House in the United States,

 there was a president named Lincoln.

He was famous for ending slavery.

 Mr. President! I know of a very capable person who could work for our government.

Oh, what kind of a person is he?

What do you think?

Did Lincoln only like good-looking people?

I am sure each person has his own values, but...

This story reminds me of the fifth donation.

For example?

A donation in which you sincerely think of others.

Well, you told me that Lincoln said he did not like that person's face. What do you mean?

I think he meant that the gentleman didn't impress him as being sincere.

Oh ...

When you face your customers, they appreciate your sincerity more than your being polite.

Donation of the heart! I never thought about it that way.

If you begin to think of your work in that way, you will be successful. I am sure of it.

I understand. I was being self-centered.

He always learns a lot.

We should practice donation.

By the way, what are the other two generosities?

They are giving up your seat to someone else, and finding shelter for the needy.

I understand. I will start with these two generosities.

Just two?

That's OK, isn't it?

That is right. Positive habits are formed, little by little.

What are you going to teach us next time?

I will talk about Precept-keeping.

Precept-keeping?

Six Paramitas That Lead to Spiritually Rich Living (Six Practices)
Precept-keeping and Forbearance

We are going to learn Precept-keeping (Devoting one's life to self-perfection) and Forbearance (being generous, patient and humble. It also means living in a positive way, even being appreciative of warnings from others).

Now I'll tell you about "Precept-keeping" and "Forbearance."

Are they teachings for self-discipline and endurance?

I'm getting a "heavy" feeling...

Don't be so serious.

But this sounds hard to do...

It sounds like not being free.

Precept-keeping certainly sounds formal and binding,

but it also means guidelines or principles, and can be part of our spirituality.

What are you saying?

In fact, don't think of it as restrictive. Think of it as a guideline for Right Living.

You mean take it in a positive way?

Yes, that's it!

For example?

Do you fasten your seat belt when you get in the car?

Of course. If I don't, I could get a fine.

If you think of the fine, you're thinking of it legalistically.

That's right, I think legalistically because I'll be fined.

But, if you think of a car accident, a seat belt saves your life, doesn't it?

I see. Thinking about my safety is not something I'm forced to do.

Yeah, that's right. Positive thinking –

What you say sounds good, but you don't practice it.

Positive thinking and the Fve Precepts...

"No killing, stealing, lying, being unfaithful to your spouse or partner, or drinking too much."

Which means not killing, not stealing from others, not having sexual misconduct, not lying, and not drinking too much, doesn't it?

Yes, that's it.

I think these five ethical precepts are more like commandments than positive thinking. I don't break them.

You've heard of people who say:

I don't kill

I don't steal

I'm not unfaithful

143

I don't lie

I promise.

I don't get drunk

Ordinary people might do some of these...

Yes, that's true.

You said there is a positive way to look at these guidelines.

Yes, for example, the first one can help you see how precious your life is.

That's positive.

Next, try to help others with their needs and keep harmony in relationships.

Speak kindly and eat healthy food.

Now I get it.

Good, can I move on to Forbearance?

Please leave it to me.

Are you sure?

Endurance is the key to my success in business.

Remember, you said some strange things about generosities?

Oh, I was mistaken, but I'm right this time.

Then let's hear it.

In business, when you hear customers complain, you have to listen to them sincerely.

And when your boss reprimands you, you can't talk back or make a face.

You just have to take it and endure it ...

What!

If you can continue to endure the boss's scolding, eventually he will stop.

That is too much stress, isn't it?

Stress is everywhere these days, it can't be helped.

Oh ...

Monk, what are you thinking?

I'd like to tell you a famous story.

About 2,200 years ago, there was a Chinese man named Han Xin. He became a great hero as a general of Liu Bang, who contributed to the unification of China.

When he was young, a bully approached him and blocked his way.

That reminds me of a story I heard when I was a kid.

Great aspirations include being able to endure.

Your interpretation might be right,

but I think that when Han Xin was a young man, he was a loner and didn't have much ambition.

He was a coward, so he endured?

No, I don't think he was a coward. He won many battles as a warlord.

Then, what made him do that?

From a spiritual point of view, it is Forbearance. He acted with compassion for the thug who was trying to give him a hard time.

The bully had not recognized his own buddha-nature yet.

How does that differ from endurance?

Forbearance is the same as compassion. It has a heart of forgiveness.

You can't help him if you get mad at him because he is a bad man.

You have to forgive people and keep reaching out to them if you are going to help them.

That is quite different from what I thought.

You just endured when your boss and customers complained,

but you should accept their complaints as good advice.

I never thought of it that way…

If you see it that way, you can improve your relationships, and eliminate stress.

When you reach that kind of mindset, your life will be rosy, right?

But if you become too exuberant, you can lose forbearance.

So forbearance is compassionate, patient, and humble.

I wonder if I'll ever get it.

Of course you will, your face is much more gentle nowadays.

You two taught me a great lesson.

We're finished with Precept-keeping and Forbearance. Now we'll study about Diligence, Meditation, and Wisdom.

Six Paramitas That Lead to Spiritually Rich Living (Six Practices)
Diligence, Meditation, and Wisdom

We are going to learn Diligence (take a steady action toward the right purpose), Meditation (have a steady mind in accord with truth that doesn't waver), and Wisdom (ability to see the True Aspect of All Things).

Let's talk about Diligence, Meditation, and Wisdom.

That reminds me how delicious vegetarian food is.

Put in your hearing aid - he said "diligence." We're not talking about food.

But it is not totally unrelated.

How?

A vegetarian dish doesn't have any meat.

Yes. It is the same as the precept "Do not kill."

If people truly put their minds to Buddhist practice, they will naturally realize the precept "Do not kill."

Is that why we eat vegetarian dishes at memorial services in Japan?

By the way, what is the true meaning of Diligence?

It means to take steady action toward a right purpose and mission.

I got it.

I'm not so sure you do.

Oh, really?

You think that I am only making money for myself, don't you?

Oh, you're not?

Is making money really that wrong?

If making money comes at the expense of others, then it is not so good. But if making money benefits others, then it is good. Don't you agree?

Glad to hear that.

Well, you said a while ago that we should make an effort toward the right purpose.

Yes, you can work diligently to follow the path of the Buddha's teachings.

In our case, what should we do?

How about practicing Donation, Precept-keeping, and Forbearance?

Indeed, we can try to be "giving" people. We can vow to perfect ourselves, be compassionate, and be humble.

That is correct.

In addition to that, everything you do in your daily life is a practice of Diligence.

Please teach us about Meditation next.

Meditation is what monks *do*, isn't it?

Isn't this the posture? The same one in which Shakyamuni Buddha reached enlightenment?

Yes, it is about sleeping while sitting up.

Don't think of it only as posturing.

But you don't call it Meditation if you lay down.

Not true. Meditation is Meditation if you are standing on your feet, or doing a hand stand.

You are joking.

You're breaking the precepts, lying!...

We learned it last time.

What I want to tell you is that Meditation is a state of mind.

Mind?

I'll tell you an old story...

In ancient China, there was an old man who lived in the countryside.

Dad! Help, help!

My horse has run away.

Is that so?

A few days later, when his horse came back, it was being followed by a magnificent looking horse.

Wow! So lucky! Now there are two horses.

But the old man smiled and said, "We will see…"

I am going to ride this horse.

Oh no!

He fell off and broke his leg.

Ouch, I am so unlucky, I can't work tomorrow.

The old man took care of the horse regardless of his disappointed son.

There's trouble! War has broken out with the neighboring land.

I heard that all young men will be drafted.

If you go to war, you won't come back alive.

Lucky me! I won't be drafted because of my broken leg.

The old man smiled as always.

That old man never gets upset.

He always works with a smile on his face.

What is the meaning of this story?

This is a very famous story. It is called "Everything in Life Is Like the Old Man's Horse."

Human beings are like horses?

It's a philosophical story.

No, it's a parable telling us not to be overly glad or sad,

because in life, everything changes.

I thought so,

but what's the connection with meditation?

There are two very important teachings in Buddhism. One is "All things are impermanent," the other is "Nothing has a separate self" (all things are interrelated).

Yes, all phenomena change, and everything is interrelated.

If you really understand this, you'll be just like that old man who didn't get upset easily.

154

I agree.

Meditation develops a quiet, steady mind that does not waver.

It is a state of mind that stays on the Path of Truth.

That's why you said to ignore posturing.

Then it's all right if I stand on my head

singing songs and eating noodles.

A person practicing Meditation wouldn't do that...

Sorry. Please tell me about Wisdom.

Speaking of Wisdom, you have plenty of it, don't you?

Yes, I studied hard in school and learned the art of making a good living.

But you don't look happy.

You are right. That's my problem.

Wisdom is nothing like school or the art of living. It's the ability to see the True Aspect of All Things.

What can I do?

Practice the Six Paramitas that you've learned.

155

Donation, Precept-keeping, Forbearance, Diligence, Meditation, and Wisdom.

If you really practice these, you will be able to handle situations much better.

Is Wisdom useful for everything?

I think so –

without Wisdom, you can hardly help others.

You mean, that's the case even for a saint like you?

Well, actually I am an ordinary man. Through my diligent practice, I received the Buddha's wisdom.

Really? Even I can do it?

We will!

Of course. Let's make every effort.

Review of the Teachings of the Buddha

Applying the Teachings to Real Life 1

application

Let's apply the teachings we have learned to our daily life.

I'm home.

What! Do you know what time it is?

Yes, but what can I do? I'm not my own boss, you know.

You're almost always late...

Well, I work hard every day. By the way, how are the kids doing?

They said they ate dinner with their friends on the way home, and went straight to their room.

That's too bad, but we all have our own lives.

I cooked dinner thinking of my family, but nobody wants to eat it.

I'll eat it tomorrow morning.

You are all so selfish!

Bang!

Oh no, she's hysterical again.

Kids! Once in a while listen to your mother and do what she says.

But all she does is complain whenever she sees me...

I don't like her telling me what to do.

I know. She can be difficult.

Good morning. How is your wife?

She is well. Almost too well.

That's good.

I have known her since she was little.

Is that so?

She's a lonely person, isn't she?

Her father died when she was small, so her mother had to go to work.

She was always alone. I used to invite her over for dinner.

I didn't know that.

I had a big family. She used to tell me that she'd like to have a family like mine.

Really?

Oh, I have to get going.

I remember now...

when we were first married, she said she wanted to have a perfect family.

Wait! I wonder if I am the "cause" of her griping?

I am going to visit the monk.

Wonderful Dharma Temple

I was thinking that my wife was wrong.

She is not happy when I go to work in the morning and she is not happy when I come home, either.

But ever since I talked with the old woman, I've been thinking of my wife's lonely childhood.

Can you see life from her point of view?

Well, I came here for your advice. How can we view this situation from the Buddha's eyes?

When a family is not in harmony there is suffering, right?

As you studied in the Four Noble Truths, there is always a cause for suffering.

If my wife isn't mad, my family is peaceful. So I think my wife is the cause.

Just her?

That's what I thought until this morning, but now I'm not so sure.

When we got married, she really wanted to make a caring, loving family.

A loving family to her meant eating meals with her husband and kids, right?

Yes, but my kids and I have not cooperated.

No wonder she stays mad...

You are now able to see things from her viewpoint, rather than just your own.

Really?

To see things this way is called Right View, which is part of the Eightfold Path.

When I reflected on my selfish ways, I began to see the real cause.

That is correct.

I understand, but what can I do?

Do you remember what comes after Right View?

I'd say, Right Thought, Right Speech, etc.

You've changed your selfish way of thinking, and value what you've realized.

Why don't you honestly tell her what you are thinking?

It's a little embarrassing, but I will show her what I recognize in her.

You've noticed. Please share your thoughts with her.

Thank you very much. I will try my best at home.

Kids! Dinner time!

I am busy.

I know, but let's eat while the food is warm.

Wow. Everybody is here today!

I'm sorry I was so selfish and didn't think of your feelings.

Let's be more careful with each other.

What's going on?

Well, your mother was lonesome when she was a child.

Her dream was to make a good home with a joyful family.

Oh, we didn't know that.

I realized that I was being selfish.

I am sorry that I stayed angry;

I was trying so hard to build a good family. I was not thinking of your feelings.

Mom and Dad are different today...

I like this –

Wow. A grown man can change.

You kids! Don't make fun of adults.

This is great, but what changed your mind?

I visited a monk. He taught me a lot of things.

Can I go with you next time?

Of course.

Good.

Review of the Teachings of Buddha

Applying the Teachings to Real Life 2

Game Center

Let's go to the game center.

But it's late.

You're antisocial.

If you don't go with us, I am not going to rescue you when bullies come after you.

Besides, you get more allowance than we do.

We need you to come with us.

I have to pay for you guys?

What did you say?

Nothing...

Oh, it's really late. My mom's going to be angry.

He was coming home early for a while but now he is late.

I'm home.

What have you been doing? You're late.

Well...

"Well" has nothing to do with it. You were out late.

You don't study or help out, and you're late for dinner.

She complains all the time...

166

You know I'm not just complaining, I'm worried about you.

You're worried about me?

Of course! You won't be able to get into a good university

or get a good job if you act like this.

Your room is a mess and you listen to loud music till late at night. What's the matter with you?

Mom, you're always telling me what to do!

It's just plain, common sense!

Not for me! I have my own ideas…

Don't talk back to me! Do your homework!

I'm leaving! I don't want to see your face!

Just a minute!

What is going on?

He left!

He's acting up.

Did you snap at him?

It's for his own good - I didn't know he's so out of control.

Kids are like that, weren't you that way, too?

Not at all –

Mom is late again.

Dad, why did you die so young...

If I had siblings, I wouldn't be lonely.

Nobody worries about me.

Thinking back, I acted up, too.

How come you look so worried?

Do you think I was too hard on him?

I know you were concerned about him, but...

Where did I go wrong?

The other day, I heard about the Ten Suchnesses at the temple.

What are they?

In short, the present situation reflects your state of mind.

His coming home late or acting up has something to do with my mind?

Yes. You can look at the situation from the Dharma of Causation.

I wonder if pushing my ideas on my son was the Cause? With that mindset, I talked to him (Condition).

The Effect is that he rebels and then we argue.

You are both feeling bad (recompense).

To start with, I must become a mother who can think of his feelings.

The son came home.

Oh! You scared me!

I have been waiting for you.

Why? You're not done complaining?

No, I talked with your Dad a while ago, and I've been thinking about things…

Like what?

I wasn't thinking about your feelings because I was caught up in my own thoughts. That's why I didn't really listen to what you wanted to say.

There's nothing I want to say...

But, what's the reason for coming home so late?

Well,

the bullies are bad - but home is worse.

Your father and I have realized that we need to see things from your point of view.

So I won't scold you if you don't listen to me, but please tell us honestly what's on your mind.

Really?

Now I know why you came home late, but why don't you like school anymore?

There is something I want to do...

What is it?

I want to be a dairy farmer.

Oh...

Honey, what are you mumbling?

Well, you – you have...

Mom, I think you expect me to become a successful business man, but that's not my dream.

So! That is why you could not concentrate on your studies.

You know even if I study hard, I can't get in to the university I want.

I'm sorry that I was forcing you in the wrong direction.

I'm sorry I can't make your dream come true.

He is thinking of you, honey. But don't you agree that he should pursue his own dream?

Yes! Please tell me more about it.

The family's conservation went smoothly.

Let's go to the game center.

Let's go home.

171

If you don't go with us, you'll have to face the bullies alone....

You know, you need us.

But it's not good for you to use other people's money.

What's wrong with you?

Our parents will worry if we come home late.

I talked with my parents and they really are concerned about us.

You're like a totally different person.

I started thinking about my parent's feelings.

I am going home.

Should we go home, too?

Yeah!

This student's emotional growth became a good influence on his two friends.

172

Review of the Teachings of the Buddha
Applying the Teachings to Real Life 3

Director, Mr. Sakai of the business department has requested an advance on his pay.

Should I go ahead and pay him as usual?

I guess so,

but wait – first, let's hear what he has to say.

But we usually…

I just want to know why he needs his pay in advance.

OK.

That's funny. He usually lets us do that without any fuss.

He used to say "employees are disposable,

so I don't care if a worker has money problems."

I heard that you wanted to see me..

I am worried about you. I just want to know the reason for the request for advance pay.

Well, I need money for this and that... I get short sometimes.

I know, but there are others who have families and can make ends meet. Why are you always broke?

There are things I want to buy, and I need money for dates with my girlfriend.

Why don't you wait until you get paid?

Do I have to wait? It's not good for my mental health.

Besides, It looks bad if I have to wait until I get paid to have a date.

Why don't you go Dutch treat?

She suggests that quite often, but I have my pride, you know.

You're short on funds because you are conceited.

Well, are you going to give me the money, or not?

174

I once heard a similar story at the temple.

If you aren't going to give me an advance, then I'll go to a loan shark.

Just wait a minute.

Monk, you taught me that making a profit is a good thing, didn't you?

That was when we were learning about Diligence.

In Right Livelihood, from the Eightfold Path, we learned how to use money correctly.

Right Livelihood?

Yes, these days it means how to live well.

Yes, I remember. Right Livelihood means to earn a living by doing something worthwhile and living within one's means.

It means to make a living in a way that does not cause trouble or harm to others or society.

Indeed, , making money while benefitting others is good.

And it is important to know how to use money after you get it.

What? I can spend my money any way I want to, can't I?

There is a line from a sutra that tells the best way to spend your money.

Yes, I remember. I wanted to tell you the words from one of the sutras.

Uh-huh.

The sutra was written to make people happy.

Spare me the lecture.

Just listen.

Well, I'm just listening, that's all.

First, you decide on a skill and use that skill in a right way to earn a living.

Then divide the earnings four ways: 1/4 is for daily living, 1/2 for business, and save the last 1/4 for a rainy day.

So what's the point?

The ratio of spending one's earnings is different for each person, but the teaching is to use the earnings with a plan. If you can do this, you will be happy.

I understand, but my date can't wait.

Are you dating Mitsuko in the business department?

Yes.

Do you want to marry her?

I asked her, but she still hasn't said yes.

I treat her and give her gifts, I'm trying hard...

I see.

176

What's the big deal today? You usually give me the advance without any questions.

I wonder if I'm really helping you by giving you the money in advance.

You usually don't care so much about employees.

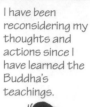

I have been reconsidering my thoughts and actions since I have learned the Buddha's teachings.

Good for you, but I'm not interested.

Everything in this world is connected, you know. The teaching says: "Nothing has a separate self."

In other words, if you are happy, the people around you will be happy, too.

My life has been good. I am happy.

Are you sure you are happy, if you're always broke and your girlfriend won't agree to marry you?

That's why I have to spend my money on her.

I have a feeling that she is worried about your free-wheeling habits.

I don't think so...

I have an idea.

What?

Ask her to wait until payday for your next date.

If I do that, she will dump me.

Just try it – if that causes a problem, come to me tomorrow. OK?

I give up.

Don't go to a loan shark –

I'll see.

Director!

Good morning, did you tell her yesterday?

Yes. It was really weird.

How?

I talked to her just like you suggested, and she didn't get mad.

Do you mind if I take you out for dinner after payday?

OK.

Are you sure?

You don't have the money for it now do you?

Right, but I'm breaking our date...

That's OK. I'm glad that you didn't borrow the money.

Why?

I was kind of worried about your spending. I feel bad when you borrow money for our dates.

But I did it for you—

A man who makes ends meet is dependable. A man who can live within his means has security.

You mean I have been doing things that made you uncomfortable?

Yes. Let's talk some more and enjoy our coffee.

Director, it was just like you said. The reason she was hesitant to marry me was my attitude toward life and money.

I thought so—she is very serious and honest.

 That's why she told me the truth, right? I guess so.

 Thanks, Director, you are a great man. Don't mention it.

 I will be honest and work hard. Please continue to guide me. Bye!

 He is happy, but I am even happier,

  because I have become someone who thinks of others' well-being. I have helped someone turn his life around.

 I thank the Buddha for this.

Review of the Teachings of the Buddha

Overall Review

Thanks to the Buddha's teachings, my life and my company got better.

That is good. What part of the teaching impressed you most?

The Ten Suchnesses. After I learned the Dharma of Causation, I was able to talk to my family.

For me, it is Self-reliance and Reliance on the Dharma.

Yes.

What is it?

We used to lean on other people.

But now we can see things differently through these teachings.

To me, it is "All things are impermanent." I thought that my family would never change.

But Mom, when you made the effort to change yourself, everyone in our family changed.

No matter what, everything is interconnected. That is the most important teaching.

What is that round thing?

Oh, that is the earth in my dream.

In the solar system everything was interconnected and in harmony. But because of me, it scattered in all directions. That is why I think "Nothing has a separate self" is the most important teaching.

Well, when we learned the Four Noble Truths, the teaching of the Ten Realms of Being Found in One Another impressed me the most. We can get from the realm of hell or hungry spirits into the realm of heaven or enlightenment, by our state of mind.

I was thankful to learn the Dharma of Twelve Causes and Conditions, as I could seek the cause of suffering.

We thought Right View and Right Thought from the Eightfold Path were the best.

Thanks to that teaching, we reflected on our self-centered views, and now we are living a happy life considerate of each other.

We also think the Eightfold Path is best, especially Right Speech and Right Action.

I agree, because of that teaching, we became good friends.

Everyone's got their favorite...

Indeed, for me it is the Six Paramitas.

Yes, Donation and Diligence, right?

What's this? Before, you said "All things are impermanent" was the most important thing.

That is true - our whole family changed.

No, no, that's nonsense. It's "Nothing has a separate self!"

It's because you don't know the teaching of Twelve Causes and Conditions, that you can be so idealistic.

What do you mean "idealistic"? Like I said, the Ten Suchnesses is it.

Self-reliance and Reliance on the Dharma, that's the one!

For me it's, Ten Realms of Being Found in One Another.

No matter how you look at it – the Eightfold Path – Right View and Right Thought.

Nothing Has a separate Self

Right View, Right Thought

Six Parami-tas

Ten Such-nesses is the best.

The Dharma of Twelve Causes and Conditions

Self-reliance and Reliance on the Dharma

The Ten Realms of Being Found in One Another

What's all the commotion?

Oh, you came just at the right time. These people aren't making any sense.

Calm down. Please tell me what's going on...

As a matter of fact...

...

I see that all of you understood a part of the teaching, but you're not grasping the whole thing.

What do you mean by "whole"?

Shakyamuni Buddha thought that everyone could see the truth by eliminating self-centeredness.

And he taught according to each person's ability to understand and put it to use.

Therefore, in this book it appears that you've learned many kinds of teachings, but what Shakyamuni Buddha was trying to teach is one principle.

One? It seems like there's more than one.

I'll summarize with an illustration.

185

Extinction

Tranquil state of mind, suffering extinguished.

Nirvana Is Quiescence

Cause

Find the root cause of suffering and reflect on it.

Ten Suchnesses / The Dharma of Twelve Causes and Conditions

Human beings cannot get out of the suffering world, if we don't understand the Truth.

Everything is suffering.
Living, getting old, sickness, death are suffering.
Parting with loved ones is suffering.
Meeting one whom you hate is suffering.
Not getting what you want is suffering.
The five aggregates are suffering.

What an illustration.

What a surprise.

Now I see the whole picture.

The lessons that everybody was talking about were all parts of the Buddha's teaching. That is why if you apply the teaching, naturally you get good results.

However, if you just understand or experience part of it, you may think "that's all there is to it." So it's not right if you force your ideas on others.

Just like we're doing…

I'm embarrassed.

It is very important to stay on the Path by studying hard in reference to the illustration on the previous page.

Let's live today fully, so that today's happiness is linked to tomorrow.

Thank you very much, monk. We could truly understand this time.

Epilogue
Three Guideposts in Life
(Taking Refuge in the Three Treasures)

It's getting dark.

Let's go home.

"Cardinal..."

What are you talking about?

Oh, there are so many things to remember. I forgot what I was saying.

You were talking about a cardinal, a pretty green bird with a big bill.

No, I wasn't!

Then what were you talking about?

I was talking about the cardinal principle of Buddhism – Buddha, Dharma, Sangha. And by the way, you were imagining a finch, not a cardinal!

How long have those words been around?

Since Shakyamuni Buddha's time in ancient India.

In Shakyamuni Buddha's time, you had to go to the Buddha and get his permission to study with him.

World-honored One, someone is at the door. He wants to become a monk.

Bring him, I want to meet him.

Time passed and the teachings spread far and wide. A personal encounter with Shakyamuni became very difficult.

Since our organization has become so large, we too, must teach.

190

But what shall we do about the rules for those wanting to be monks?

It is impossible for the Buddha to see each one of them.

But it is not good to let a person be a monk if they don't have a firm commitment.

World-honored One! What kind of person should be accepted as a monk?

A person who can take refuge in the Three Treasures.

What are the Three Treasures?

Buddha, Dharma and Sangha, right?

Taking refuge in the Buddha. Taking refuge in the Dharma. Taking refuge in the Sangha.

Anyone who is determined to keep these three is qualified to be my disciple.

This is called Taking Refuge in the Three Treasures.

Grandpa, what do you mean by "taking refuge"?

Sangha means having a close connection. Buddha gave this name to an assembly of people, who walk on the same path – those seeking to Awaken.

Oh, the assembly of Buddhists.

You're not taking this seriously –

Well, compared to the Buddha and the Dharma, it's not that important.

Not true…

World–honored One, I think "Taking refuge in the Sangha" is only half as important as "Taking refuge in the Dharma."

In those days, the disciples usually asked the Buddha, "This is what I understand, what do you think?", rather than asking the Buddha the importance of the Sangha.

No, Ananda, your thought is not correct.

Did I give the Sangha too much credit?

By taking refuge in the Sangha you have achieved all of the Buddha's teachings.

All of them?

Ananda, by taking refuge in the Sangha, you can encourage one another and walk on the path together.

You can also be free from the sufferings of birth, old age, sickness and death.

Thinking of these, you can see that it's possible to achieve all of the Buddha's teachings by Taking Refuge in the Sangha.

Yes, I will wholeheartedly take refuge in the Sangha.

Without Taking Refuge in the Sangha, you can hardly take refuge in the Buddha, much less practice the teachings.

For that reason, the Sangha might be the most important of the Three Treasures.

You are so right. The most important thing to nurture in society is forming human harmony.

Grandpa, I really understood the importance of "Taking Refuge in the Three Treasures." Thank you.

It's getting dark, let's go home.

Who, who, who

Hey, how long have you been able to hoot like an owl?

That wasn't me....

Who, who, who ...

Oh look, there's an owl.

Hey, What's that you're crying?

I have been crying this since long ago.

Oh really? Why?

To remind everyone "who" to take refuge in.

How easily we forget.

That's OK. I'm happy to continue reminding everyone.

MAY 2 5 2010